AWAKENING

Awakening

Poems
by

LAURA SOLOMON

BOOKS

Adelaide Books
New York/Lisbon
2018

AWAKENING
Poems by
By Laura Solomon

Published by Adelaide Books, New York / Lisbon
adelaidebooks.org

Editor-in-Chief
Stevan V. Nikolic

For any information, please address Adelaide Books
at info@adelaidebooks.org
or write to:
Adelaide Books
244 Fifth Ave. Suite D27
New York, NY, 10001

ISBN-10: 1-949180-36-0
ISBN-13: 978-1-949180-36-7

Printed in the United States of America

Content

Awakening

I am waiting patiently for you to awaken.
You are several hours behind
And half a world away.

Perhaps it's not wise
But I do it anyway
For reasons known to my heart
But still veiled from my mind.

You say you wait for me
So we are equal
Though I do not like to keep score.

A song plays –

"You and I were almost dead"

And I think of my many close calls;

The lightning strikes, the car crash,

the surgery to the brain,

To name just a few.

Yes, seven of my nine lives have been used up –

I'm down to just two now

So I offer them up to you –

Hoping you will take good care of them.

I could now be almost the living dead,

zombie, vampire or ghost –

You could walk or see right through me;

See me walk through walls, not needing a door,

A humble boast, a sleek trick, some call it showing off.

Scars and schoolyard beatings haunt your past,

Making me afraid for your future.

Wanting it joined to mine.

We could help each other in mysterious ways;

Each manufacture half a skeleton key –

Push open every locked door,

Leaving nothing undone.

I could hand you a sewing kit –

needle and cotton thread,

You could stitch yourself a new heart –

I could make it beat in two-four time

And we could waltz

Perfect strangers who should know better.

Four Walls

Somebody is giving birth in the room next door.

Nine months is up, it's time for the big arrival.

The rest of us are pregnant with the future –

Pregnant with possibilities

Each one opening out – a door to

walk though, an invitation.

The midwife arrives bearing oxygen

Which is not needed

More pushing is done,

The umbilical cord is cut – time's up,

Three kilos of perfection is delivered.

Geography

They were both prisoners of their minds.
"You don't have to be a solo driver", she said to him,
Hoping to lighten his heart.
He claimed it had the desired effect -
At least some of the time.

Both of them bore battle scars.
Soldiers in the field, they stood shoulder to shoulder,
Facing the same way – a cold wind blew
As they stood staring into the midday sun
Just after that last eclipse.
He reassured her fears with his constant words –
And a miniature universe was born.

The phone lines between them were clear;

No crackle, no static.

Except for on one occasion

When he was speaking and she

could not hear his voice –

Which was disturbing.

She admired his tenacity -

He kept on trying to get through.

She made a map, and he stuck coloured pins on it,

Markers to mark where they had been,

And also where they were going.

They could not see the edge of the map.

He told her he wanted to be a land surveyor

So she sent him a book on topography,

Along with the latest MRI scan of her brain.

Together they explored the geography

Of their strange and unexpected new love.

The Doctors

The doctors know it all, know best,
Know whether to wait or operate,
When to lock you up or set you free
And how much walking time you shall be granted.

I am at their mercy, or I was,
And hope to never be again.
They have no knowledge of compassion.

What terrible power!
Power of life or death.
One slip of the surgeon's blade and it's curtains;
Or paralysis – the wheelchair, or walking with a cane.

The nurses aren't much better,

They gossip amongst themselves, scatter-brained,

Mocking my ambitions,

While they have none of their own.

This whole episode must be a set-up

Engineered by some malicious god

Playing a prank on me.

Who will have the last laugh?

The cackle's stuck in my voice box,

From upstairs I can hear

Somebody else having a giggle

At my expense;

I am happy to provide the entertainment.

Mind you, at the risk of sounding like a know-it-all,

It must be said that back here on earth

None of them can tell me

Why it grew – this monstrosity

This tumour

This lump inside my head.

The Party

You have to be dead to be invited to this party.

As is to be expected, all the stars are here.

Janis, Marilyn, Jesus.

There are ordinary people too though.

Kevin Watson who died of a blood clot to the brain

shortly after his 40th birthday.

He's been resurrected. Now he's

partying in the corner –

he's put himself in charge of the music

and is playing Nirvana

as Cobain toys with a segment of his blown-off head.

Other run-of-the-mill folk present?

Jimmy Molesworth who hung himself

and is now hitting on Janis Joplin who is oblivious
to the attention, dancing wildly to Come As You Are
a whisky bottle clutched tightly in her right hand.

Jimmy's still got rope marks around his neck.

There's Cindy Rutherford who was hit by a car
while simultaneously cycling and listening to her iPod.
Not a good combination. She's got splinters of glass
from the windscreen embedded in her face.

Marilyn decides to re-stage her death
for our general entertainment.

She strips off and swallows a bottle of pills.

Then passes out in the bed. Nobody looks alarmed.

It's all faked; we can't die now that we're dead.

The black telephone rings.

I move to answer it.

Nobody is there.

I can hear the 22nd Century heavy

breathing down the line.

The Swarm

It was spring. There was competition.
The bees had been busy manufacturing new queens.
They sat in their special cells, waiting to hatch.
The first to hatch was mated and
became the chosen one.

Two females cannot live in the same hive.
The old queen flew away, taking
half the swarm with her—
Her dedicated followers.

She searched for a hollow tree or a hole in a wall
In which to make a new home.

Success—that old tree across the road—
The perfect place to build.

Her half of the swarm settled down with her—
The rest remained behind.

And so a new life was made—
A new existence forged.

The ousted set up her own hive
And never looked back.

Animal Instinct

Man or animal?

Well what have we here –

A near perfect stranger getting kicks for free

Every night like some Cobain song

while I march along in time,

No doubt just as guilty.

I'm old enough to be his mother, there's

something twisted about that,

I ask myself why I continue - nobody

has an answer to this question.

It's trauma that makes the story great,

The wider yawns the abyss, the greater shines the glory,

Think of all the medals we could hang upon our walls,

Polished and shining, public display - if

you care for that sort of thing.

Gloss up your scars until they gleam

– then put them up for sale,

There's a space now where they operated,

Must be my lucky day - my mind plays tricks on me,

Not knowing which door to open,

Behind this one a candy store, behind

that, a hard brick wall,

The sands of deception shift and

change - as everything dissolves.

A limited life span brings everything into focus,

People they care for me,

Well, don't tell me I'm living beneath my dignity,

As other humans serenade with

songs I can no longer hear

All my circuits are cut off.

Kiss goodbye to your old way of living,

You too can dwell in cripple's alley,

Thinking only doomed thoughts,

That back you into a corner, get

you up against the wall –

Shrug and kick it off –

Song plays 'There's an empty space inside my heart'

The road stretches on ahead of us –

Into something that resembles infinity.

Returning to the Table

After some time I return to the table.
I check the corridor in both directions
To see if it is safe.

Are my myriad enemies, my detractors,
Hiding behind chairs,
Ready to spring out and lacerate me for fun?

It's like shooting bullets at a ghost.

Here I come, down the main corridor
Like the marshmallow man in *Ghostbusters*
Destroying buildings and roads,
My footsteps leave no trace on the floor.
Only dust in my wake.

I hear echoes from further down the hall;
The coast's clear. Come on out. Come on out and have fun.
Don't let the bastards grind you to nothing,
Forget about what they done –
Here it is, your space at your table,
The chair pulled out waiting for you to take a seat.

My leaden limbs fall foot after

heavy foot upon the floor.

My face is paralysed; my tongue frozen in my head.

What the hell am I going to say?

I sit and wait for the word, an angel at this table,

The page remains as blank as snow, you know,

What the hell am I going to...

I pick up the pen and make a dark red mark, an X.

It's all I have to say to you,

The one who will come after,

The 'yes' after the 'no',

Cover your hair and your eyes,

Drive on through the darkness,

Drive on through the night,

Stay long enough in the blackness,

And the dark will turn to light.

The Sword
Swallower's Lament

They promised me the blades wouldn't

be too sharp – they lied!

Yes, throat cut to ribbons, it's true.

Though it's best always

To spare gory details

And focus instead on my outfit.

Yes the outfit!

See how it sparkles and shines.

The boob-tube covered in seq uins

Catches the light from a certain angle.

The hot pants are velvet

And covered in yellow stars -

A birthday gift from my mother.

They say that I look the part.

Always pays to make an effort.

A girl needs dreams.

And stars, too, not just on my bum,

But also shining in my eyes,

At least there used to be.

Once they lit up like dollar signs,

Or at least that's what other people saw,

When they looked,

Which wasn't very often.

Now my grin's turned rather cynical

But the main thing is – electricity -

The whole house hums with it -

A superior supply

It keeps all the appliances happy

And just as long as nobody

Gives you a mains belt

Everything should be sweet.

The swords?

Now they were handed down from my grandfather

Hattori Hanzo – the finest steel.

They say mine is a spectacular show

that draws the cheers.

At the end of the night;

Here sit I – my bloodied stomach,

My lacerated throat.

After the Surgery

Nobody warned me
about the boredom.
So much time on my hands -
Great Dali-style melting clocks worth of it.

And wanted nowhere, shunted from pillar to post
Within the health care system.

What am I meant to do with my days post-surgery?
Sit around staring at blank walls,
Hang out at the local drop in centre,
Take respite in the country.
Fresh air and plenty of it – that's the ticket, so they say.
Quiet desperation is the Kiwi way -
Ten years left, take it day by day.

Solitary

Four walls closing in
Why do they do this to us?
Dragged from cell to cell,
It's a form of torture,
a form of abuse.

Lock them away
When they lose their minds
We don't want the monsters taking over,
Hush, keep them quiet,
Tie them up, tie them down,
Lord it over,
Teach them who's boss.

That's the ticket.

And if they escape,
Climb over the fence,
Make a run for it?

Heaven forbid!

Punish them twice as heavily.

Rules are rules
And must be respected.

This place is based on the army.

Everything is regulated,

Even the meals

Which are served on paper plates

With plastic cutlery

We wouldn't want anybody cutting themselves

And giving themselves an injury.

It's never pleasant -

Trouble in the mind.

This is the only way we could see

To deal with it.

We were frightened

Of what we did not understand,

So we put a label on it,

Gave it some drugs

Shoved it into the corner

And hoped it would go away.

It did not die.

Locked away

It grew stronger.

As a tree deprived of nutrients

Will sometimes become more hardy

In order to survive.

Our plan failed.

Solitary was banned
Much to our chagrin.

The United Nations
Had a lot to do with it.

They called it torture
And human rights abuse
Which is only
Speaking the truth.

We hate people who tell the truth.

We believe they should have
Their tongues cut out.

Give us docility any day of the week,
Happy pleasantries are what we like -
How's the weather and
How are the kids.

Familiar territory we know and love.

Now it's back and we're terrified.

Kauri

Strong trunk,

Strong branches,

Native to New Zealand -

Growing tall,

Your likeness

Hangs upon my wall.

Was it a walk in the forest

That inspired this painting?

Just looking at it

Brightens my day,

So heartening to have

Native trees

Upon the wall.

Your gum was used as a fire starter.
Your timber had many uses.

Mighty tree
I look at you
take heart.

Building Wharf

'I don't knock myself out' he said.
'Mostly I just tinker.'
He was at it for six months.
The wharf was a monolith -
a construction made of wood and plastic
that jutted out into the water.

My father is an engineer -
the wharf bore the hallmarks of his design.
It floats upon the water -
And will float there after his death,
A momento.

It's something for his grandchildren
to play on
or dive off if they are game enough
into the murky waters
down, down, into the tangled weeds.

It's an entity for the ducks to perch on
squawking to each other
in their own special language
duck-speak, unintelligible
to the human ear.

My father takes pride in the wharf

It's a retirement achievement

A man needs hobbies

To keep himself busy

We all know what happens

To idle hands

Heaven forbid

The devil should take his

At this stage of life.

I made a special trip

to the family farm

to see the wharf

to find inspiration for this poem.

I found what I was looking for.

A poem in the form of a jetty.

Jutting out into the water -

Solid for generations to come.

Eternal Summer

It's the snowy depth of winter
I'm seeking an eternal summer.

One that can't be taken away.
Give me something to hold on to.

My novel's being born.
A long slow process,
High hopes find
A more realistic path.

Young dreams smashed

By the world

In middle age I continue

After major surgery

And a solitary cell

Still I'm at it.

Word after painful word

Is penned and sent away

My hopes rest on emails

I'm sending you a summer

Complete with bluebells,
Swallows and a burning sun.

Bask in it. Pray it lasts -
To see you through
Your own dark, dry season.

About the Author

Laura Solomon has a 2.1 in English Literature (Victoria University, 1997) and a Masters degree in Computer Science (University of London, 2003).

Her books include Black Light, Nothing Lasting, Alternative Medicine, An Imitation of Life, Instant Messages, Vera Magpie, Hilary and David, In Vitro, The Shingle Bar Sea Monster and Other Stories, University Days, Freda Kahlo's Cry, Brain Graft, Taking Wainui, Marsha's Deal and Hell's Unveiling.

She has been short-listed in Bridport, Edwin Morgan, Ware Poets, Willesden Herald, Mere Literary Festival, and Essex Poetry Festival competitions.

She was short-listed for the 2009 Virginia Prize and the 2014 International Rubery Award and won the 2009 Proverse Prize. She has had work accepted in the Edinburgh Review, Orbis and Wasafiri (UK), Takahe and Landfall (NZ). She has judged the Sentinel Quarterly Short Story Competition.

Her play 'The Dummy Bride' was part of the 1996 Wellington Fringe Festival and her play 'Sprout' was part of the 2005 Edinburgh Fringe Festival.

www.ingramcontent.com/pod-product-compliance
Lightning Source LLC
LaVergne TN
LVHW091233080426
835509LV00009B/1260